LIBRARY SMARTS

KNOW THE PARTS OF A BOOK

JANET PIEHL

Lerner Publications Company • Minneapolis

For Cameron Madsen

Lerner Publications Company
A division of Lerner Publishing Group, Inc.
241 First Avenue North
Minneapolis, MN 55401 U.S.A.

Website address: www.lernerbooks.com

Library of Congress Cataloging-in-Publication Data

Piehl, Janet.
    Know the parts of a book / Janet Piehl.
        pages   cm.— (Library smarts)
    Includes index.
    ISBN 978-1-4677-1501-0 (lib. bdg. : alk. paper)
    ISBN 978-1-4677-1751-9 (eBook)
    1. Books—Juvenile literature. I. Title.
    Z116.A2P54 2014
    002—dc23   2013004884

Manufactured in the United States of America
1 – CG – 7/15/13

TABLE OF CONTENTS

A Book about Frogs

Will loves frogs. He goes to the library. He looks for a book about frogs.

Will spots the book he wants. How does he know what the book is about? Will knows the parts of a book.

The Outside of a Book

Will looks at the **spine**. The spine of the book is its smooth thin side. The spine holds the pages together.

The title of the book is on the spine. It shows the word *Frog*. The author's name is on the spine too. The **author** is the person who wrote the book.

Will looks at the book's front cover. He sees a picture of a frog. He sees the author's name.

Will wants to know more about the book. He looks at the back cover too. The main ideas of the book are written on the back cover.

The Inside of a Book

Will opens the book. He turns the first page. He comes to the title page.

The title page lists the title, the author, and the **publisher**. The publisher is the company that made the book.

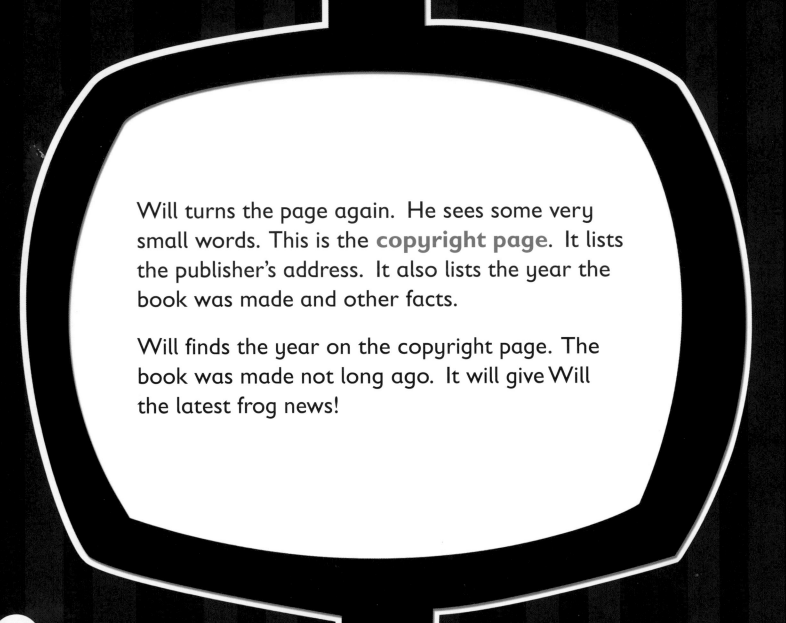

Will turns the page again. He sees some very small words. This is the **copyright page**. It lists the publisher's address. It also lists the year the book was made and other facts.

Will finds the year on the copyright page. The book was made not long ago. It will give Will the latest frog news!

...ner Publications Company
A division of Lerner Publishing Group, Inc.
24... st Avenue North
...olis, MN 55401 U.S.A.

...address: www.lernerbooks.com

... Congress Cataloging-in-Publication Data

...an, Buffy.
Can you tell a frog from a toad? / by Buffy Silverman.
    p.   cm. — (Lightning bolt books.™—Animal look-alikes)
Includes index.
    ISBN 978-0-7613-6732-1 (lib. bdg. : alk. paper)
    1. Frogs—Juvenile literature. 2. Toads—Juvenile literature. 1. Title.
QL668.E2S546 2012   2011000688
597.8'9—dc22

Manufactured in the United States of America
1 – CG – 7/15/11

Getting around a Book

Will wants to know if frogs lay eggs. He looks at the next page. It is called the **table of contents**.

The table of contents lists the chapters in the book. It also tells what page each chapter starts on.

One of the chapters is called "Egg Time." It starts on page 22. The chapter tells about frogs laying eggs! That is what Will is looking for!

Will turns the pages. He sees the page numbers. They are at the bottoms of the pages. He goes to page 22.

Egg Time

Female frogs and toads both lay eggs in the springtime. They lay their eggs in puddles, ponds, and streams.

Frogs lay clumps of eggs. The eggs are covered in jelly. Other animals eat most of them.

Clear, thick jelly covers and protects these frog eggs.

Will sees the chapter title at the top of page 22. It says, "Egg Time." He is in the right place!

Will comes to a word he does not know: *tadpole*. The table of contents lists a **glossary** at the back of the book. It is on page 30.

A few frog or toad eggs hatch into tadpoles. Tadpoles live in shallow water. These baby frogs and toads breathe with gills. Tadpoles don't have legs.

Tadpoles breathe through gills like a fish.

Toads lay long chains of eggs too. But some survive. Predators eat most of these eggs.

He turns to page 30. The glossary tells him what the new word means. A tadpole is a young frog.

Will reads the whole book. He liked the part about frog skin. How can Will find that page again?

gland: ~~a body~~ chemicals

insect: an animal that has six legs and three main body parts as an adult

lung: a body part that some animals use for breathing air

mucus: a thick liquid that some animals make to keep their skin moist and protect it

predator: an animal that hunts and eats other animals

tadpole: a young frog or toad that has hatched f~~rom~~ an egg

a bump on a toad's skin

webbing: a thin layer of skin between an animal's toes

Frog ~~a~~
http://www.um
arml/frog_cal'

National Geo
Everything
http://vided
animals/ar
bull.html

National
Red-Eye
http://k
creatu

Ryder
Life
Hen

Sil
Mi

He finds the **index** at the end of the book. The index lists many topics in the book. It tells what pages they are on. He turns back to the pages about skin.

Will knows all about frogs. And Will knows all about the parts of a book!

Index

Photo Acknowledgments

The images in this book are used with the permission of: © Matt Antonino/
Shutterstock Images, p. 1 (top); © Jaimie cross/Shutterstock Images, p. 1 (bottom);
Adam Gryko/Shutterstock Images, p. 2; © Joel Sartore/National Geographic/Getty
Images, p. 4 (top); © ElectroArt/Dreamstime.com, p. 4 (bottom); © PhilSupapherStock,
pp. 7, 8, 9, 12, 17, 19, 22, 24, 25, 26, 28 (top right, center left, bottom right); © Jozsef Szasz-Fabian, p. 28
(top left); © Chris Mattison/Alamy, p. 13; © Dwight Kuhn, pp. 14, 16;
© Oxford Scientific/Photolibrary, p. 11; © Michael Durham/Minden Pictures, p. 18;
Images, p. 5; © Gerry Meszaros/Visuals Unlimited Images, p. 2; © Animals Animals, p. 15
(top left); © Eric Isselee/Shutterstock Images, p. 16 bottom right); © David Kuhn, p. 18; © James Bowen.
io; © Eric Isselee/Shutterstock, p. 25; © Jabben573/Dreamstime.com, p. 27 (top); © Dr. Keith Wheeler/Photo Researchers,
pp. 23, 28 (bottom left); 30; © FilmJI/Shutterstock Images; © Eric Isselee/Shutterstock Images
Dreamstime.com, pp. 27 (bottom); 30: © Eric Isselee/Shutterstock Images

Front cover: © Arco Images GmbH/Alamy Images (top);
(bottom).
Main body text set in Johann Light 30/36.

GLOSSARY

author: the person who writes a book

copyright page: the part of a book that tells facts about the publisher. It also tells when the book was published. The copyright page is usually at the front of a book.

glossary: the part of a book that tells what new or important words mean. The glossary is at the back of the book.

index: the part of a book that lists the topics in a book and the pages where they are found. The index is at the back of the book.

publisher: a company that makes books

spine: the smooth thin side of a book

table of contents: the part of a book that lists each chapter and what page it starts on. The table of contents is at the beginning of a book.

INDEX

Photo acknowledgments: The images in this book are used with the permission of: © Todd Strand/Independent Picture Service.

Front Cover: © Brian Summers/First Light/Getty Images.

Main body text set in Gill Sans Infant Std Regular 18/22. Typeface provided by Monotype Typography.